DON'T KISS UNTIL...

TRICIA GREENWOOD

Foreword

Let me sit with you for a minute...
Not as an expert.
Not as someone who's figured it all out.
But as someone who's walked through it too.

Let's walk through it together.

— Tricia Greenwood

Table of Contents

CHAPTER 1

It's About Your Heart

Love feels like magic. It can sweep you off your feet with laughter, warmth, and moments that make your heart race and your spirit soar. The spark of connection can fill you with hope, joy, and the beautiful possibility of sharing your life with someone who truly sees you.

That feeling, the flutter in your chest, the smile that won't fade, the warmth in your breath, is real and precious. Love is one of the most wonderful experiences life offers, and your heart is designed to open and respond to it.

But alongside that magic, love also asks for care and wisdom.

You don't need a psychology degree to know when something feels off. That little nudge in your gut? It's not paranoia, it's your intuition trying to protect you. In love, ignoring that whisper is often where even the smartest, kindest people lose their way.

When you meet someone new, the conversation flows effortlessly. They make you laugh, see you in a way you haven't been seen in a long time. Then comes the kiss, sweet, surprising, maybe even electric. You catch yourself smiling afterward, imagining all the possibilities.

But here's the gentle truth: it's not the kiss itself that puts you at risk; it's your heart.

Our minds are powerful storytellers. Sometimes, our imagination paints a picture of the future so vividly that we begin to believe in a story that hasn't fully unfolded, a connection that's more hopeful than real. That's why it's so important to count on your inner voice, your intuition, the quiet, steady compass guiding you through the noise.

It's not the lips that carry the weight; it's the emotional investment that often comes too fast. When we give that part of ourselves before it's been truly earned, it's we who end up paying the price.

We're taught to set physical boundaries, to not go too far too soon. But what about emotional boundaries? Why don't we talk more about those?

Because you can hold your physical line and still let someone slip into the deepest parts of your heart before they've shown who they really are. And that's how you end up heart-worn by someone who knew exactly what to say but vanished when it got real.

The deepest ache doesn't come from the kiss itself; it comes from handing your heart to someone who didn't know how to hold it.

And it's not foolishness that leads to this, it's hope. We want so much to believe the spark means something. When loneliness has settled in, a little attention can feel like sunlight after a long, cold winter.

But not everyone who lights you up is meant to stay. Some are just passing tourists in your life; some are distractions dressed up as destiny.

Before you start imagining forever, take a deep breath.

Ask yourself:
– Have they shown you consistency, or just charm?
– Do you feel emotionally safe, or just

momentarily excited?
– Are they truly curious about who you are, or only enjoying being admired?

Kisses are easy. Real connection takes time.

So go slow. Guard your heart without apology.

Not because you're cold, but because you're wise.

The right one will wait, and when they do, it will be worth it.

CHAPTER 2

Behind the Screen

There's something strange about dating in the digital world, isn't there? You can talk to someone every single day, share funny posts, late-night thoughts, even those vulnerable little pieces of your heart, and still not truly know who you're talking to. Because texting chemistry isn't the same as a real connection.

Words typed on a screen can be edited, rehearsed, even borrowed from someone else. And it's so easy to project what we *hope* someone is, rather than seeing what's there.

Before your heart gets too involved, I want to gently encourage you, hear their voice.

A real voice tells you so much more than any message ever could. You can feel energy in their tone, or a lack of it. You can sense kindness... or something controlling. You'll notice hesitation, sincerity, confidence, or even that strange feeling in your stomach that quietly says, *something's not right.* Pay attention to that feeling. It's your body whispering wisdom.

And if you ask to talk and they avoid it, or always have an excuse not to call, that's important. A person who truly wants to connect won't hide behind a screen. They'll want to be seen. And they'll want to see *you.*

But I need to be honest with you, there's another reason to be careful. These days, too many good people are being taken advantage of. And it's not because they're foolish. It's because they're kind... open-hearted... hopeful.

I've seen it happen. To women who thought they met a devoted single dad stationed overseas. To men who fell for someone who claimed to be a sweet widow just looking for a fresh start. They shared dreams and they believed their story. And then came the requests: a travel emergency. A frozen bank account. A child who needs help. Just a little something to get through the week.

It feels small at first. But suddenly, you've given not just your heart, but your trust, your time, your peace of mind... and maybe your money.

If this has happened to you, please hear me: **It's not your fault.** Scammers don't just lie, they *study*. They use empathy like a trick mirror, reflecting what you most long to hear.

It doesn't mean you're naïve. It means you care. It means you're human.

But next time, and there *will* be a next time, because love is still out there, I want you to pause. To check in with yourself. Not out of fear, but out of love... for *you*.

Real connection will never be afraid to show up. Real love doesn't ask you to send money or carry guilt. Real people speak. They call. They *want* you to know who they are.

So please, don't fall in love with someone's messages. Don't get attached to the fantasy version in your mind. Instead, pick up the phone. Listen to their voice. Notice how you feel when they speak. Not just your heart, your nervous system. That quiet, honest place inside that always knows.

You are worthy of the kind of connection that doesn't disappear when you need it most.

Someone who truly wants you won't stay behind the screen. They'll show up. And when they do... you'll feel it. Something in you will soften and exhale and say, *"Yes... this is different."*

CHAPTER 3

The Truth in Their Past

When you're on a first or second date, it's easy to get swept away by excitement. There's something quite thrilling about discovering someone new, the spark of connection, the laughter, the shared stories that feel like the start of something beautiful. But beneath the surface of that excitement, there's a quieter, wiser voice inside you. It nudges you to pay attention, to look beyond the surface, to listen carefully when your date begins to talk about their past relationships.

How someone speaks about their exes, their previous loves, and those chapters of heartbreak isn't just small talk; it's a window into their emotional world. It's one of the first places you can glimpse their maturity, their ability to grow, and their readiness for something real.

People often say that actions speak louder than words. But when it comes to past relationships, words and how they're spoken can reveal just as much, if not more, than what someone does. It's in the way they frame those experiences, the emotions that ripple through their voice, and the fleeting expressions on their face.

Pay close attention to the tone. Does their voice soften with fond memories, or harden with resentment? Do their eyes light up when they remember the good times, or do they flicker with pain or anger? Sometimes, the eyes tell the story even when the mouth tries to smooth it over.

You might notice a smile that doesn't quite reach their eyes or a quick glance away when they mention a particular person. These subtle clues are like emotional fingerprints, unique and revealing. It's okay to feel curious about these signals, but don't let them pull you into judgment. Instead, hold space for their whole humanity, knowing that everyone carries wounds and stories they're still learning from.

Another key aspect is how they take responsibility, or don't. Notice if their stories consistently place blame elsewhere. Do they talk about their exes as villains or monsters? Or do they show a willingness to reflect on their part in what went wrong? Emotional growth shines through when someone can say, "I made mistakes too," or "We both had things to work on."

On the flip side, if every past relationship is painted as a disaster caused solely by the other person, it's a red flag. It may suggest that they haven't done the work to heal or learn, and that pattern might repeat itself. Watch for a tone of bitterness or defensiveness; these can be warning signs that they're still carrying unresolved hurt that could affect your connection.

It's also common to hear vague reasons like "we just weren't right" or "things didn't work out." While those might be true, listen carefully to the pauses and hesitations around those statements. Sometimes what isn't said reveals more than what is. Are they avoiding details? Do they change the subject quickly? These moments can hint at stories they're not ready to share yet, or things they might not fully understand themselves.

As you listen, notice their body language. Do they lean in as they speak, open and engaged? Or do they cross their arms, look down, or seem closed off? Facial expressions, furrowed brows, tight lips, nervous smiles, can tell you how comfortable they really feel sharing these stories. Trust your instincts about whether their vulnerability feels genuine or rehearsed.

Navigating conversations about past relationships doesn't mean grilling someone or hunting for dirt. It's about creating a space where honesty can flourish naturally. You might say gently, "What's something you learned from your last relationship?" or "How do you think your past has shaped what you want now?" These questions invite reflection without pressure.

Remember, everyone's healing journey looks different. Some people find it easy to talk about the past openly; others need more time. What's important is that they show a willingness to be real and take responsibility for their emotional growth.

Early dates are about more than chemistry; they're your chance to see emotional maturity in action. How someone processes their history speaks volumes about how they'll handle future challenges, conflicts, and joys with you.

So, when the stories of "the one that got away" or "why it didn't work" come up, pay attention. Listen not just to the words but to the feeling behind them. This isn't about judging a person by their past, it's about understanding if they're someone who's ready to build a healthy, honest connection.

You deserve someone who can talk about their past with grace, someone who acknowledges their mistakes and celebrates their growth. Because the way they speak of their past shapes the story you might share together.

And that story? It's worth listening to carefully.

CHAPTER 4

Their Space, Their Life

Imagine yourself soaring high above someone's life, like a bird gliding effortlessly over their world. From this height, the small details blur, but the patterns come into sharp focus, the rhythm of their days, the shape of their space, and the echoes of their habits painted across the landscape below.

You see their home nestled like a secret garden. Is it a place tended with care, where sunlight streams through clean windows and flowers bloom? Or is it a wild tangle of weeds and forgotten corners, where shadows linger and dust gathers like memories left unspoken? The state of their space isn't about perfection; it's a reflection of their self-respect; a silent story told in every shelf and surface.

Drifting closer, you peer inside. The living room breathes life or holds stillness. Are cushions plumped like gentle clouds, inviting you to rest? Or are they hidden beneath towers of forgotten things, like autumn leaves piling up in a forgotten forest? The kitchen counters speak too, are they sparkling with the promise of shared meals, or cluttered with the relics of rushed mornings and postponed intentions?

Now, your gaze falls on their car, a vessel that moves through the world carrying more than just a driver. Is it a clean chariot ready to carry you both into new adventures, or a cluttered nest weighed down by lost dreams, fast food wrappers, and the ghosts of undone errands?

This mobile space is a mirror of their inner landscape, revealing whether they carry emotional baggage packed tight or travel light with open hands.

From this lofty perch, you feel the invisible currents, the energy of a life well-ordered or one tangled in forgotten knots. Someone who loves themselves enough to care for their world moves through it like a careful gardener, pruning, clearing, and nurturing growth.

They understand when to hold on and when to let go, facing storms instead of hiding beneath piles of debris.

As you glide above, ask yourself gently:
"Is this a place where my spirit can breathe and my dreams can take root? Or am I descending into a whirlwind of unfinished business and quiet chaos?"

You deserve a partner whose inner garden is as lovingly tended as their outer world. Someone who carries their burdens with grace, not someone whose life feels like a tempest you're called to calm.

From this vantage point, the first signs of readiness shine like lanterns on a foggy path, the care they put into the small corners of life whispers who they are deep beneath the surface, and how gently they might hold the space you both will share.

This isn't about chasing perfection; it's about seeing with clarity. It's about finding someone aware and awake, ready to grow, to let go, and to love deeply, both themselves and you.

CHAPTER 5

Dreams and Reality

When you're trying to figure out if someone's truly ready to build alongside you, it helps to notice how they live their words every day. Do they show up for the little things, the bills, the appointments, the promises? No one's perfect, and we all stumble sometimes, but steady effort matters more than grand dreams without follow-through.

Listen to how they talk about money, work, and responsibility. Are they open and honest, sharing struggles as well as small wins? Or do they dodge the topic, get vague, or blame outside circumstances? Someone ready to grow faces tough conversations honestly, even when it's hard.

Look at their energy. Are they motivated to try, even when things get messy? Or do they seem weighed down, caught in overwhelm and excuses? There's a difference between needing a break and choosing to stay stuck.

When setbacks come, and they will, observe how they respond. Do they breathe, seek solutions, and ask for help when needed? Or do they spiral into blame or denial, leaving you to carry more than your share? Real growth comes from facing problems, not hiding from them.

If you want to know where someone's at, ask gentle questions like, "What's something you're working on right now?" or "How do you like to handle your finances?" Their answers reveal their mindset, not just their plans.

Be honest about your own values and habits too. Sharing what matters to you opens the door for real conversations and mutual understanding.

If you notice a pattern of avoidance or inconsistency, set boundaries early. You might say, "I want to support you and your dreams, but I also need to know we're both contributing and managing our responsibilities."

And trust yourself. If your gut says their words and actions don't match, don't ignore it. Your intuition is there to protect your heart and time.

Dreams keep hope alive, but it's daily discipline, steady steps, and willingness to grow that build a future worth sharing.

Now, if someone you care about is facing health challenges, physical, mental, or emotional, that can add complexity. Health struggles don't make them less worthy of love; often, they show strength and resilience. But energy may fluctuate, and progress can be slow or unpredictable.

If things seem promising, start by being a true friend. Listen without rushing to fix. Support without taking over. Celebrate small victories and respect when they need space.

At the same time, protect your own boundaries. Supporting someone through health issues doesn't mean sacrificing your well-being or taking on their responsibilities. Love with care but honor your own needs.

Notice how they manage their health journey. Are they seeking help, making positive choices, staying open to growth? Or stuck in denial or avoidance? Their willingness to work on their well-being matters just as much as any other responsibility.

Love in these moments requires patience and compassion, but also honesty about what you can give and need in return. Walking beside someone through health struggles can be beautiful if both of you show up with respect, care, and clear communication.

No matter the challenges, you deserve a partnership where effort and accountability are shared, and where your dreams and well-being are honored alongside theirs.

CHAPTER 6

Watch How They Treat Others

This might be one of the most important chapters in the entire book.

Real love isn't just about how someone treats you when things are easy. It's about how they treat others when there's nothing to gain.

Start with how they talk about their family. Is there tenderness, even in complicated relationships?

Do they always show respect or blame? If someone constantly badmouths their parents, especially their mother, that unhealed resentment doesn't stay buried. It will show up again, eventually, with you. Are they judgmental?

If they have a pet, especially a dog, watch that too. It's not about being a "dog person." It's about how they treat a living being that depends on them. Do they show affection, responsibility, care? Or is it irritation and neglect?

Because someone who struggles to love the ones who love them unconditionally... may not have the capacity to love you when you're not at your best.

And then, of course, the waitstaff.

This is one of the clearest windows into someone's character.

Go out to eat. Watch what happens when the order is wrong. Do they stay kind? Do they say "please" and "thank you"? Or do they roll their eyes, act entitled, or get short with someone just doing their job?

People who are rude to service staff aren't just "having a bad day." They're showing you how they behave when they think no one important is watching.

And that behavior will not stay confined to strangers. It will show up in your relationship too, especially when stress hits.

Bonus tip: listen to how they talk about their exes. If every person they've dated was "crazy," "toxic," or "the problem," be careful.

Someone who's never taken responsibility for their part in past relationships is likely to repeat the same mistakes and make you the next one to blame.

You don't need someone perfect. You need someone present. Someone kind. Someone who treats everyone with humanity, not just the people they want something from. Because how they treat their mother, their dog, the waiter, and their past, tells you exactly how they'll treat you when the excitement fades and when real life sets in.

And you, my friend, deserve consistent love, not just charm.

CHAPTER 7

Who Do They Call?

You can learn a lot about someone by watching who they call when life gets hard.

Not just who they text funny posts to or make weekend plans with, but who knows them. Who's seen them at their lowest and didn't walk away?

Friendships, or the lack of them, reveal more about someone's emotional maturity than you might expect.

It's easy to confuse popularity with connection. A person can be surrounded by people and still feel completely alone. Just ask yourself: do they have close, meaningful friendships? One built on trust, time, and truth?

Do they have people who challenge them when they're off course, who hold them accountable, and who have stood beside them through both good and hard seasons?

Or are their "friends" just surface-level companions, fun on Friday, gone by Monday?

There's a difference between bonding over drinks and building community. Real friends tell you the truth. They call you up, not just out. They don't just celebrate your wins; they walk with you through your shadows.

And here's something important: if someone has never had a deep friendship, guess who ends up being their first emotional support system?
You.

Suddenly, you're their therapist, their cheerleader, their accountability coach, all wrapped into one. And while that may feel sweet at first, it becomes exhausting fast.

Healthy relationships thrive when both people already know how to connect.
Not when one person is teaching the other how to care.

Take a quiet look at their social circle. Who have they chosen to surround themselves with?
Are their people kind, grounded, thoughtful?

Or are they careless, chaotic, or constantly unavailable?

You don't have to judge their friends, but don't ignore them either. They're a reflection.

Because someone who's never shown up for others consistently probably won't know how to show up for you.

And someone who has never been accountable to anyone may eventually resent being accountable to you.

Before you get swept up in the connection, ask: When life gets messy, who do they turn to? If the answer is "no one," then be careful, because one day, it might all fall on you.

CHAPTER 8

What's In the Fridge?

It might sound funny at first but take this seriously: the inside of someone's fridge can tell you a lot about how they live, and what kind of life they're building.

Open the door and peek in. You're not just looking at what they eat. You're looking at how they nourish themselves, how they plan (or don't), and whether they show up for themselves in the small, quiet ways that no one sees.

Are there real groceries in there? Leftovers in containers? A jug of water, some fruit, maybe even a veggie or two?

Or is it takeout cartons, expired milk, energy drinks, and ketchup packets from 2021?

It's not about being fancy. This isn't a test for chefs or meal preppers. It's about care. Intention. A baseline of self-respect.

Because if someone doesn't have the capacity, or the desire, to care for their own body and space in small ways, what will happen when they're called to care for a relationship?

If they're always unprepared in their personal life, chances are, they're not quite ready to build something lasting with someone else. It might be easy to overlook when chemistry is strong. But fast forward six months. Are you doing all the grocery runs, all the cooking, all the clean-ups?

That stops feeling romantic real fast.

Someone who feeds themselves well, even in simple ways, often lives with care. They offer you a drink before you ask. They know your favorite tea. They make space for you not just physically, but emotionally.

The next time you visit, take a glance, not to judge, but to understand.
Are they preparing for love... or waiting for you to clean up the mess?

CHAPTER 9

Can They Handle "No"?

Let's talk about something tender, how someone handles your "no."

Too many people know the feeling: you set a simple boundary, "Not tonight," or "I'm not ready for that", and suddenly everything shifts. The mood darkens. They get quiet. And you're left wondering if you did something wrong.

You didn't.

Saying no shouldn't make you feel like the bad guy.

Someone healthy will respect your "no." Even if they're disappointed, they'll listen. They'll lean in. They'll stay kind.

But someone who sulks, withdraws, or tries to guilt you into changing your mind?
That's not sensitivity. That's emotional manipulation.

Pouting is subtle. It doesn't always look dramatic. Sometimes it shows up in silence, sarcasm, passive-aggressive comments, or the dreaded "fine."

But underneath it all is pressure.
The message being sent is: "Your boundary hurt me, and now you have to fix it."

And over time, that pressure starts to train you. You begin to say yes when you don't want to. Not because your heart changed, but because you're trying to avoid the fallout.

That's not love. That's survival.

The right person won't make you feel guilty for honoring your own limits.
They'll hear your no and thank you for your honesty.
They won't pull away or punish you.
They'll stay, stay soft, and seek to understand.

Because to someone who genuinely cares about you, a "no" isn't rejection, it's trust. You trusted them enough to be real.

You should never have to manage someone's emotional reactions just to keep the peace. That's not your job. That's not intimacy. That's emotional labor that will drain you.

So set your boundaries. Speak your truth clearly and calmly.

Then watch what happens next.

How someone responds to your "no" reveals more about your emotional safety than their best compliment ever will.

You deserve someone who honors your words. Not someone who pouts when they don't get their way, but someone who grows, listens, and stays.

Because real love doesn't diminish you. It makes room for your full truth.

CHAPTER 10

Words or Actions?

Let's have a real moment here, just the two of us.

Words can be beautiful. They can sweep you off your feet, light up your imagination, and make you feel seen and wanted. Compliments, promises, and dreams about the future all sound good. And maybe, like so many of us, you've been touched by someone's words in a way that made you believe it was the real thing.

But here's the truth that time teaches you: words without action are just noise. Even the sweetest sentences mean nothing if the follow-through is missing.

It's not about perfection. It's about effort. Integrity. Consistency.

You know what it feels like when someone says, "I'll call you later," and then disappears. Or when they say, "You can trust me," but something inside you stays tense. And over time, you start to notice the pattern. The promises sound the same, but you're the one left holding it all together. And it wears on your heart.

You start doing the emotional labor. Making the plans. Being the reminder. Justifying their behavior to yourself or others. Hoping maybe they didn't mean to forget. That maybe next time will be different.

But love shouldn't make you question your worth. Or cause you to feel like a project manager trying to keep things on track.

Someone who genuinely values you will not leave you guessing. They'll show up, without being asked. They'll remember the little things. They'll follow through not just because they said they would, but because they want to be the kind of person whose word can be trusted.

It's not about grand gestures. It's about consistency.

It's how they respond when you're not feeling your best. When you need emotional space. When you say, "not tonight" or "I'm overwhelmed." That's when their real character shows up.

Do they get quiet, passive-aggressive, or try to guilt you into compliance?

Or do they listen, and ask for what you might need, offer a blanket, a moment, a bit of grace?

Because anyone can say they love you. But only someone who respects you will honor your boundaries.

Love isn't proven in poetry. It's proven in patterns.

You don't need someone who talks like a dream and moves like a ghost. You deserve the kind of love that shows up without needing applause. The kind that holds your hand *and* holds their promises.

You don't need someone who talks like a dream and moves like a ghost. You deserve the kind of love that shows up without needing applause. The kind that holds your hand *and* holds their promises.

When Someone Says, "I Don't Lie" All the Time...

You will likely notice how strange and how often the people who say "I don't lie" are the ones who often lie the most.

They say it like a badge. Like it makes them instantly trustworthy. But here's the truth: real honesty doesn't need to advertise itself. You feel it. You see it in the way someone shows up, stays consistent, and owns their actions, even the messy ones.

If someone keeps insisting, *"I don't lie,"* repeatedly, just ask yourself: Why do they feel the need to say that so much? Are they trying to convince you or themselves?

Sometimes it's overcompensation. Sometimes it's deflection. Sometimes it's a subtle manipulation tactic to shut down your gut instinct or make you feel guilty for questioning them.

True honesty doesn't puff its chest. It doesn't need to remind you every five minutes. It just lives in the way someone acts, day after day.

So don't be fooled by declarations. Look for consistency. Look for quiet integrity. Look for the person who tells the truth even when it's inconvenient, even when it might cost them something. That's the kind of honesty you can trust.

And if someone must keep telling you who they are... it might be because they're not showing you.

Take a moment to check in with your heart, gently and honestly. Do they follow through on what they say they are going to do, or do you often find yourself left waiting, wondering, hoping? Do their words line up with their actions, or are you always trying to bridge the gap between what you were promised and what you receive?

And most importantly, how does your body feel around them? Do you feel calm, steady, safe, or do you find yourself tensing, second-guessing, shrinking just to keep the peace?

Real love brings a kind of quiet reassurance. It doesn't stir up chaos or confusion. It brings ease to your spirit and peace to your nervous system.

CHAPTER 11

Real Plans or Just Talk

It's easy to get swept up in sweet words about the future. Perhaps they have mentioned to you about traveling together, building a life, and starting a family someday. They say things like *"when we..."* or *"us"* and *"forever,"* and it makes your heart soften.

It feels beautiful to be imagined in someone's future. But then, time passes... and not many changes. The words are still there, but the action. Not so much.

Maybe they get quiet when you try to talk about next steps. Maybe they shrug off making plans, saying they're just "figuring things out" or "waiting for the right time." At first, you're understanding. You give them space. But slowly, that dreamy future starts to feel more like a stall tactic than a shared vision.

You begin to wonder if they really mean it, or if they just like the comfort of having you nearby while they stay undecided.

Here's something you need to remember, no matter who you are: talking about the future is not the same as *building* one. It doesn't mean you need to rush into anything or demand a ring tomorrow. But it does mean you deserve someone who moves toward you with intention.

Someone who makes space in their world for you, not just in their words, but in how they show up, how they plan, and how they prioritize you.

People can be unsure. People can be scared. But if you find yourself always the one holding on, waiting for them to get ready, ask yourself: *Is this love... or limbo?*

Because someone who truly sees you as part of their life will move with quiet confidence, even if it's slow. They'll take your hand, not just talk about a future but begin walking toward it with you.

Check in with your heart: Are you being included, or just imagined? You deserve to be chosen in real time, not just someday, but now.

CHAPTER 12

Time as a Form of Love

Time is one of the simplest, most powerful ways we show love. When someone shows up when they say they will, it tells you: "You matter. I respect you. I thought about you."

But when someone is chronically late, always canceling, or full of excuses, it can wear on you. You begin to feel like an afterthought, even when they don't mean to make you feel that way.

Sure, life happens. Traffic. Emergencies. Everyone gets overwhelmed now and then. But when lateness or flakiness becomes a pattern, it's no longer about circumstances. It's about priorities.

Do they remember your plans? Or are you sitting alone, checking the time, feeling unsure? Do they communicate clearly when things change, or do they vanish until it's convenient again?

One-off slip-ups are forgivable. But repeated carelessness is a signal.

Because when someone is careless with your time, they're often careless with your heart.

And while we're here, how do they respond when you don't feel up for something? Whether it's conversation, a date, or physical intimacy... do they pause and offer care? Or do they guilt you, pout, or pull away?

The people who truly care won't rush you. They'll ask, "What do you need?" They'll stay kind, even when they're disappointed.

Because real love doesn't demand. It responds.

Ask yourself: Do they make excuses or try to try? Do they take your time for granted, or treat it like the gift it is?

Because someone who shows up on time is showing you more than punctuality. They're showing you they're ready. For life. For love. For you.

CHAPTER 13

Genuine or Love Bomb

At first, it feels amazing. They say all the things you long to hear: "You're incredible."
"I feel like I've known you forever."

Texts come pouring in, late-night calls stretch into the early morning, and before you know it, you're swept into a beautiful vision of a future together, even before they know your middle name.

It's intoxicating. You feel seen. Wanted. Alive.

But then... something shifts.

The messages are slow. The calls stop. The warmth fades. And suddenly you're left wondering, "Was it all in my head?"

It wasn't. You felt something real, but maybe they didn't.

This is what people call love bombing, not love.

Love bombing is like fireworks that explode too quickly, bright, dazzling, but gone before you can catch your breath. Someone comes on too strong, too fast, showering you with affection and promises, not because they're ready for a real connection, but because they're chasing a high or trying to control the story.

It feels like intimacy, but it's really a mask.

You're not being loved for who you truly are, you're being idolized for what you represent in that moment.

If this has happened to you, hear me when I say: it's not your fault. You didn't imagine it. But it also wasn't love.

The real thing, the kind that lasts, is different. It moves slowly. It respects your pace. It listens when you say "no" and never rushes you.

Love builds. It waits. It shows up day after day, even after the fireworks have faded.

Not all love bombers are cruel; some aren't ready for real intimacy. They crave closeness, the excitement of connection, the rush of being seen and desired, but when it comes to the deeper, more vulnerable parts of a relationship, they hesitate or pull away.

It's like standing at the edge of a pool, wanting to dive in but afraid of the cold water beneath. They love the thrill of the surface, the laughter, the flirting, the butterflies, but real intimacy means diving deeper, letting their guard down, and showing parts of themselves that feel fragile or imperfect.

That kind of closeness requires courage, courage to be vulnerable, to risk disappointment, to face fears of rejection or loss. For some, those fears are too big or too familiar, so they keep the connection at arm's length. They'll come close enough to feel the warmth but not close enough to get burned.

This isn't your fault. It's not because you're not lovable or not enough. It's simply their level of readiness. They might be wrestling with their own past hurts, insecurities, or a fear of being truly seen.

Sometimes, they confuse intimacy with losing control. They fear that if they open their hearts fully, they might lose themselves or be judged. So instead, they love in flashes, big gestures, intense emotions, but no lasting foundation.

And it can feel confusing and painful for you, because their presence is magnetic but inconsistent. You catch glimpses of who they could be, but the distance remains.

It's important to recognize that their hesitation isn't a reflection of your worth. It's a reflection of their journey, a journey they may not be ready to take yet.

And that awareness can be freeing. It allows you to hold space for their fears without taking them on as your own. It reminds you that you deserve someone willing to meet you fully, who's ready to dive deep alongside you, not just skim the surface.

When you encounter someone like this, it's okay to protect your heart and your pace. Love is a partnership, and both people need to be willing to grow and lean in.

You deserve steady love, the kind that stays, that embraces both your light and your shadows, and that builds a safe place for your whole self.

One of my friends, Jenna, shared her own experience with me. She met someone who seemed perfect, so attentive, so charming. But when she asked to slow down, to get to know each other, he disappeared. "It felt like being caught in a whirlwind, beautiful and terrifying," she said. "But real love, I learned, is like a quiet fire. It warms you slowly, steadily."

If someone starts talking about "forever" too soon, take a breath. Step back. See how they respond when you ask to slow down.

Someone who truly sees you will honor your pace. They won't need fireworks or grand gestures to prove it. They'll simply show up, steady and kind.

That's love, not just the flame, but the warmth that stays.

These days, marriage looks different from it did for our parents or grandparents. More people wait until their late twenties or thirties, when they feel ready, settled, and surer of themselves.

That's a good thing. Taking your time means you marry from a place of clarity, not pressure.

Even though "forever" can feel overwhelming, here's some hope: divorce rates are going down. About forty to forty-five percent of marriages end in divorce, which sounds high, but it's less than in decades past.

People are more careful now about who they say "I do" to. They're spending more time really knowing each other before making that lifelong promise.

Of course, no relationship is perfect. Couples face struggles, miscommunication, money worries, and drifting apart. But what matters most is how you face those struggles. Can you listen? Can you grow? Can you keep choosing each other day after day?

About forty percent of marriages now include partners who've remarried, bringing lessons and hopes into new beginnings.

Technology and online dating have changed the way people meet, giving us new paths to find someone who truly clicks with our hearts and values.

But before you dive fully in, here's a gentle reminder: put your family, your faith, and your own well-being first. These are the anchors that keep you steady when the seas get rough.

When you build your love on that foundation, it has the space to grow steady and strong.

As the writer Bell Hooks said, "Love is an action, never simply a feeling." She defines "real love" as an action rooted in care, commitment, and responsibility, rather than just a feeling. It involves nurturing both one's own and another's spiritual growth through acts of care, respect, knowledge, and assuming responsibility.

And as you walk your own path, remember: "The best love is the kind that awakens the soul; that makes us reach for more." (Nicholas Sparks)

Numbers and trends give a broad picture, but every relationship is its own unique story.

What matters is entering love with honesty, care, and a willingness to grow, not just for today, but for the journey ahead.

CHAPTER 14

How Fast is Too Fast

This one's tender and deeply important.

We don't always say it out loud, but there's a quiet truth many of us carry that our bodies are more than skin and shape. They're keepers of our energy, memory, and emotion. They carry our stories, our instincts, our "yes," and our "not-yet."

Whoever you invite near should understand this isn't just about attraction, it's about trust. Your body is a sacred space. And how someone treats it tells you everything about how they value you.

Some people want intimacy quickly. Not because they've earned your heart, but because they crave closeness without the commitment.

They want the rewards without the time to really know each other...

They press forward because it makes *them* feel wanted, without pausing to ask how *you* feel. Sometimes it sounds like charm. Sometimes it comes cloaked in compliments. But if it feels like pressure, it is.

Rushing is not good chemistry. Real chemistry doesn't push, doesn't demand, and doesn't play games with your boundaries. Real chemistry feels Safe, Alive, Mutual.

When someone truly respects you, your boundaries aren't a problem; they're a gift. They don't see your "no" or "not yet" as a hurdle to overcome or a challenge to their ego. Instead, they hear it as an honest expression of who you are in that moment, and they honor it with kindness and care.

They don't make you feel like you owe them long explanations or justifications for your feelings. They understand that your boundaries come from a place of self-respect and trust, and that respecting those boundaries is the foundation of real intimacy.

You won't catch them acting like there's a line of others waiting for their attention, making you feel like you must compete for your place in their heart. Their focus will be entirely on you, not on winning or conquering, but on creating a space where you feel safe, valued, and truly seen.

They'll want your peace far more than just your presence or your body. Because to them, closeness isn't a prize or a victory, it's a sacred connection that deserves gentleness.

In their eyes, your comfort matters more than their desires. They'll pay attention to your words, your silences, your smallest gestures. They'll notice when you're unsure or hesitant, and they'll respond with patience, not pressure.

It feels different when someone truly respects you. Your heart relaxes. Your breath slows. You don't have to pretend or perform. You can simply be.

And that kind of respect isn't just about this moment, it's a promise for all the moments to come.

And if they don't? If they pout, pull away, or guilt you for not "giving more"? That's not love. That's a red flag with flashing lights.

Let's talk about something few people do: the science of bonding.

There's a quiet difference between love and lust, and it's one that your heart already knows deep down.

Lust takes. It pulls you in with heat and hunger, craving the rush, the thrill, the moment. It's loud, demanding, and sometimes overwhelming. It wants to possess, to consume, to have without giving back. Lust is often about what feels good right now, about filling a space inside with excitement, not connection.

Love, on the other hand, gives. It's patient, gentle, and steady. Love shows up not because it needs something, but because it wants to offer everything, kindness, understanding, respect. Love is about holding space for someone else's heart, even when it's messy or complicated.

Love listens when you speak, even if what you say is hard to hear. Lust hears only what it wants to hear, filtering everything through desire.

Love asks, "How can I support you?" Lust asks, "What do I get?"

Love celebrates your joys and holds you through your pain. Lust is there only for the highs, fading when things get real.

Love grows by giving itself away freely, expecting nothing in return but the chance to be known deeply. Lust grows by grabbing and clinging, never satisfied, always needing more.

You've probably felt the pull of both, and it can be confusing because lust feels so intense, so alive. But love is the quiet power beneath all that fire. Love is what stays when the flames settle down and the world is just you and the other person, raw and real.

When love is true, it lifts you up. It doesn't take away your light, it makes it shine brighter.

So, when you find yourself wondering if what you feel is love or lust, ask yourself: Is this feeling giving life to my soul? Or is it draining my peace? Is it asking to know all of me, or only the parts that thrill?

Love waits. Lust rushes. Love sees you. Lust sees what it wants.

And your heart, your wise, beautiful heart, already knows the difference.

When you're physically intimate with someone, your body releases powerful chemicals, **oxytocin, dopamine,** and, for men, **vasopressin.** These aren't just pleasure responses. They're bonding agents. They tell your brain, *"This person is safe. Stay connected."* They create a sense of emotional attachment, even if the relationship isn't emotionally safe.

Over time, if you connect too deeply with partners who don't stay, your body and brain can become confused. The bond forms... then breaks. Again, and again. And eventually, it becomes harder to trust those bonding instincts. It's not your fault. It's biology. And it's why we must sometimes slow down, not out of fear, but out of self-respect.

There's something else, too. New studies suggest that **the memory of physical connection lives in your cellular structure.** Your body remembers who's been close. Not just emotionally, but **physiologically.** This doesn't mean you're "damaged" if you've had multiple partners. It means your body carries echoes. Imprints. And those echoes matter.

When you take your time now, when you pause before offering that part of yourself again, you're not being "difficult." You're being wise. You're protecting something sacred. You're saying, *"I've learned what connection means to me. And I'm choosing it carefully this time."*

And if someone walks away because you didn't give them what they wanted? Let them. Let them go knowing they were never meant to stay. That wasn't rejection, it was **revelation.**

You deserve to be **honored**, not handled. You deserve someone who sees your **entire being,** not just your body. You deserve **slowness, safety, and sincerity.**

From now on, let your boundaries reflect your healing, not your hurt. Let your pace be led by your wisdom, not your fear. And let the next person who comes close be the kind of soul who doesn't rush love but reveres it.

CHAPTER 15

Money Habits Matter

Let's talk about money, not from a place of judgment, but from a place of care. Because when we're talking about love and partnership, money isn't just a side note. It touches everything.

Money is energy. It's how someone shows up in life. How do they take care of themselves? How they plan, or don't plan, for the future. And most importantly, it's how they handle pressure, responsibility, and accountability.

It doesn't matter how much someone makes. Truly. What matters is how they live with what they have.

Are they wise with their resources or constantly living on the edge of their credit limits? Do they avoid talking about bills, spending, and savings, or can they have an honest conversation without flinching?

It's not about being perfect. Life happens. People lose jobs, go through divorces, or face emergencies. Debt, in and of itself, doesn't make someone reckless. But what matters is how they respond to those seasons. Do they learn? Adjust? Ask for help when needed? Or do they pretend everything's fine while silently drowning in chaos?

Many people these days live off credit cards, postponing consequences in favor of appearances. They keep swiping to maintain a lifestyle, not because they can afford it, but because they don't want to look like they're struggling You can't build a future with someone who's pretending to live in the present.

It's easy to be charmed by someone who treats you to expensive dinners or gives flashy gifts. But if their account is in overdraft and they're dodging calls from creditors, that's not generosity, it's escapism. And escapism is not a foundation for real life.

Even more concerning? When someone makes *you* feel like it's your role to fill in the gaps. If you're always the one covering bills, lending money, or "just helping out this once" (again), take a breath. Ask yourself gently: **Am I being appreciated, or am I being used?**

Because love without boundaries becomes imbalanced. And financial imbalance, when ignored, turns into quiet resentment.

If you're the one who earns more, or plans more, or always foots the bill to keep things going, pause. Check in with your heart. **Is this mutual, or are you slowly carrying more than your share out of hope, guilt, or fear of losing them?**

You deserve a partner who *wants* to build something solid with you, not just enjoy what you've built on your own.

And if you're currently in a season of financial struggle yourself, this isn't a rebuke. It's a call inward. Start where you are. Make one small change at a time. The point isn't to have it all figured out, it's to be honest, aware, and committed to growth.

Because someday, whether you're single, in love, or newly married, you'll be facing real-life moments. Roof repairs. Hospital bills. Groceries. Gas prices. Retirement. Emergencies you didn't plan for. Vacations you dreamed of. Legacies you want to leave.

If someone can't plan for tomorrow, they're not ready to walk into it with you.

Financial maturity is not shallow. It's emotional safety. Money itself doesn't define a person's worth or goodness. But how someone handles their finances, their honesty, responsibility, and respect around money, reveals so much about their character.

It shows how they manage challenges, how they plan for tomorrow, and most importantly, how they'll treat what's yours: your time, your trust, your heart.

When someone shows care with their money, it's a sign they value stability, respect boundaries, and are willing to share responsibility. And that creates a foundation where love can grow without fear or uncertainty.

CHAPTER 16

Are They Truly Available?

We don't talk enough about what it's like to be on that emotional rollercoaster with someone who keeps you off balance. You know the type, the person who's charming and attentive one minute, then suddenly distant and unreachable the next. They say all the right things, make you feel wanted and special... and then they vanish, cancel plans last minute, or dodge any real conversation about what you two even are.

At first, that unpredictability can feel exciting. Your heart races, and every text or call feels like a small victory. But over time, the excitement wears off, anxiety creeps in, and starts to color everything. You find yourself obsessing over every word, rereading old messages, and doubting your instincts.

Sometimes, this kind of behavior isn't just about being emotionally unavailable; it's about being dishonest. When someone keeps you guessing this much, it's worth asking if they're truly free to give you their whole heart. Are they hiding parts of their life? Are they still involved with someone else, maybe a spouse or a girlfriend/boyfriend, while telling you otherwise?

Dishonesty like that is painful, but it's better to face the truth than stay stuck in confusion and hope. Someone who's juggling multiple relationships can't offer the honesty, respect, or commitment you deserve. Their mixed signals might be their way of covering up secrets, and that emotional push-and-pull is a warning sign, not a romantic mystery.

Here's the truth: someone who keeps you guessing isn't mysterious or complex, they're just inconsistent. And inconsistency? It's not romantic, it's draining.

Real love isn't a puzzle you have to solve or a game you must win. It's peace. It's the quiet knowing that when they say they'll be there, they will be. It's the feeling that you don't have to tiptoe around their moods or guess what they're thinking. It's the space where you can simply be yourself without fear of losing their attention.

If you find yourself constantly chasing their affection, waiting for texts, hoping they'll call, or trying to decode their silence, you're not in a relationship. You're stuck in a loop. This pattern is like an addictive game: a little attention here, a little withdrawal there, until you're hooked, not on love, but on the hope that it might feel good again someday.

But here's the thing: you are not a slot machine. You shouldn't have to keep pulling the lever, hoping for a jackpot that never comes. You deserve better than that.

A mature, emotionally available partner won't make you guess what they mean or feel. They won't punish you for wanting clarity or ask you to settle for uncertainty. They will make you feel safe, seen, and heard, and that safety is everything.

Ask yourself honestly: Do you feel emotionally steady and secure when you're with this person? Or do you feel like you're constantly performing, trying to earn their love or attention?

You deserve someone who doesn't mistake drama for passion or confusion for depth. Someone who helps you rest in love, not someone who tests you with games or silence.

Love should never be a test you have to pass. It should be a place where your heart can relax and breathe easily.

Remember, you're worthy of a love that's calm, consistent, and caring. And when you find it, you'll know because it won't keep you guessing; it will simply feel like home.

CHAPTER 17

Peace or Chaos?

We all have moments when things don't go as planned, when there's a disagreement, a missed cue, or even just a misunderstanding. The question isn't whether conflict will arise in a relationship. It will. The deeper question is: *What do they do next? How is it handled or managed?*

Do they pause? Breathe? Ask for clarity? Or do they go straight into blame, defensiveness, or shutdown?

There's a big difference between reacting and responding. Reacting is fast. Automatic. It comes from a place of fear, habit, or ego. It's the slam of a door, the sharp word, the rolling eyes. It's interrupting before listening, accusing before asking, and storming out instead of sitting down and talking it out. Reaction is what we do when we feel threatened and haven't yet learned another way. We should only react when it's a surprise or an accident or a shock. Otherwise, we should respond.

Responding is slow. Grounded. It doesn't mean you're a doormat or that you never feel strong emotions. It means you've learned to *pause and think about what you are going to say instead of blurting out something you shouldn't.* To check in with yourself before saying something you can't take back. It means you respect yourself and the person in front of you, enough to stay curious rather than combative.

And here's the truth: emotionally respectful people don't fly off the handle every time something goes wrong. They've learned the difference between a real emergency... and a triggered ego. They don't confuse a question with a threat. They don't take every comment as an insult or every silence as rejection. Instead, they slow down. They ask, "What did you mean by that?" instead of assuming the worst.

That kind of response takes practice. Especially if you were raised around yelling, shutdowns, or people who used guilt as a tool. You might have learned that love came with drama. That passion had to be loud. That someone walking out meant you'd better chase them. You may think that those arguments were just part of being close.

But they're not.

Healthy relationships are still passionate, but they aren't volatile. You don't have to be on edge all the time. You don't have to tiptoe or talk them down. One of the most loving things a person can do is simply *stay present* when things get tense. Stay in the room. Stay kind. Stay honest.

Self-respecting people know this: it's not about *never* getting triggered. It's about learning not to act on the trigger without first checking in with your truth.

That's why responding is a skill and a gift. It means thinking before you speak. Breathing before you shout. Letting your emotions *move through* you without weaponizing them.

If the person you're with creates chaos in small moments, turns misunderstandings into explosions, or blames you for how they feel, you're not in a relationship; you're in a cycle. One that will drain you.

Ask yourself honestly: Do I feel emotionally safe around this person? Can I bring up hard things without fear of it blowing up? Do they listen with the intent to understand, or with the intent to defend? Do they make peace or stir more pain?

Because love, real love, isn't about who's louder, who "wins," or who makes the better point. It's about emotional safety. Mutual respect. And choosing peace, not drama, even when things get hard.

You are not here to fix anyone's temper. You are not responsible for calming their storms. You are not their sponge for anger, their echo for blame, or their excuse for staying stuck.

You're a human being. With worth. With value. With a heart that deserves a steady, safe connection.

And anyone who truly loves you will want to bring more peace into your life, not more pressure.

CHAPTER 18

Red or Green Flags

Love isn't always about grand gestures or perfect moments. Sometimes, it's found in the little things, like the way someone laughs at their own mistakes, or the gentle teasing that makes you smile instead of shrinking away.

This is about the true test of love: can they laugh with you, not at you? Can they bring lightness when life feels heavy? Because the way someone handles humor says so much about how safe, seen, and valued you'll feel with them, today, tomorrow, and for all the days to come.

Let's explore why laughter matters more than you might think, and how it can be the quiet heartbeat of a relationship that lasts. Let's talk about something that might seem small but speaks volumes.

What happens when you tease them gently, maybe after they put salt in their coffee instead of sugar, or forget where they parked and you both end up wandering under the sun laughing like kids? Do they smile and shake their head, letting the moment roll off their back? Or do they tighten, go quiet, bristle, or snap back with something that stings?

The way someone reacts to light-hearted teasing tells you everything about how safe they feel in themselves, and how safe you'll feel with them.

See, when someone can laugh at themselves, it's a quiet sign of emotional maturity. It means they've made peace with the fact that being human is messy and funny sometimes. They're not chasing perfection. They're not terrified of looking silly. They can trip, laugh, and get back up without needing to take anyone down with them.

And when someone can do that, when they can *laugh with* you and not take themselves too seriously, you'll find that they create a sense of safety around them. You can breathe easier. You can show your own awkward, clumsy moments without fear. Because you know they'll never use your vulnerability as ammunition. They'll chuckle, maybe tease you back lovingly, but they'll never wound you.

But there's another kind of person, and you need to watch out for them.

The one who **can't** laugh at themselves but seems to always be laughing **at you**. They hide behind a smirk and say things like, *"Relax, it was just a joke,"* when you tell them something that hurt your feelings. They make digs about your appearance, your habits, your past, then twist it into humor, acting like *you're* too sensitive for reacting.

That's not joking. That's passive-aggressive mockery. That's covert control.

And the tricky part is, it doesn't always come off as obvious cruelty. Sometimes it's subtle. It might be a sarcastic comment in front of your friends. A "harmless" jab about your weight, your age, your dreams, your family, delivered with a smile and a shoulder shrug. But you feel the sting. And you start second-guessing your reactions.

That's emotional erosion, not connection. And it's not okay.

People who are truly confident don't tear others down for a laugh. They don't get defensive when they're on the receiving end of playfulness. They don't make you feel guilty for not finding their "jokes" funny. Instead, they join in the lightness. They know when to laugh *with* you, when to hold space for you, and when to say, "Oops, my bad, that wasn't funny."

Humor should connect you, not chip away at your spirit.

And one of the most important green flags in any relationship is this: how does this person handle imperfection? Theirs, and yours? If they can smile at their own slip-ups, if they can take a joke with grace, if they don't make a scene out of a spilled drink or a wrong turn, you'll know. This is someone you can be human with.

Real love lives in those moments of shared laughter. Not performative laughter, not the laughter that masks discomfort or power plays, but the real, relaxed kind. The kind that says, "I like you, even when we're both a little ridiculous."

So don't ignore how someone handles humor. It might seem light, but it points to something deeper: whether their presence builds comfort or creates tension. Whether they tease with kindness or weaponize wit.

You deserve to laugh and feel safe at the same time.

You deserve someone who laughs beside you, not above you.

CHAPTER 19

Good Vibes or Drained Energy

Sometimes, the question isn't just about grand gestures or big moments, it's about how someone makes you feel day in and day out.

Do they bring lightness and laughter into your life, or do they leave you feeling exhausted and empty?

Do they make your spirit dance with joy, or do they quietly drain your energy, piece by piece?

Laughter isn't just a moment of fun, it's a sign of comfort, safety, and connection. When you can laugh together, especially at the little things, it means you're truly at ease.

On the other hand, when the laughter fades and tensions enter, it's worth asking yourself what's going on here?

Because love that makes you laugh is love that lifts you up in every way, while love that drains leaves you searching for a way out.

Let's explore how to recognize the difference, and how to choose the kind of love that fills you with joy, not fatigue.

You know those people who light up a room? The kind who makes you feel safe, and completely yourself just by being near them. Maybe they don't say much, but their energy wraps around you like a warm embrace. You relax. You breathe easier. You feel alive.

And then there are others, those who walk in and something just feels... off. You can't quite put your finger on it. Your chest tightens. Your energy sinks. A quiet voice inside you asks, "What just shifted?" Your spirit, your deepest self, is speaking before your mind even catches up.

Attraction can be dazzling at first, but it's energy that tells the real story. You might find yourself making excuses. "They're just having a bad week," or "Maybe I'm overthinking." But your intuition knows better. Your nervous system feels uneasy and knows.

Your soul knows. There's a difference between butterflies and warning bells. One makes your heart flutter with excitement. The other leaves you anxious, unsure, and shrinking inside.

If you're constantly tiptoeing around how to be, wondering if your happiness is too much or if your feelings will push them away, that's not love. That's a slow fading of who you are. It's exhausting in ways that touch every part of you, your body, your mind, and your spirit.

You might smile less, doubt yourself quietly, and lose touch with your intuition. Not because you're weak, but because you're pouring so much energy into staying emotionally safe with someone who may not even see the damage they're causing, or worse, doesn't care.

True love isn't about surviving the storm or managing chaos. It's a gentle sanctuary for your nervous system. A home where your voice matters, your quirks are celebrated, and your dreams find room to grow. Love that lifts you up touches your soul, grounds your energy, and helps you find your way back to yourself.

Remember, your body holds sacred wisdom, your gut feelings, your breath, your heart's rhythm aren't just physical reactions, they're messages from deep inside.

When you feel drained or uneasy around someone, don't dismiss it. That's your inner wisdom telling you to protect yourself.

If your spirit tightens, no matter how much chemistry there is, no connection can fix that.

Now, I want to speak to your strength.

Maybe you've carried more than you ever thought you could. Maybe you gave your all, managed the emotional labor, the parenting, the schedules, the bills, and yet still felt invisible or undervalued. Please know, this isn't your fault.

Strength doesn't mean shrinking or settling. It means knowing what you bring and never begging for love again.

You deserve someone who honors your generosity without taking it for granted. Someone who isn't afraid of your light but inspired by it. Someone who shows up, not with empty promises, but with presence, respect, and peace.

Choosing to love now means choosing from a place of power, not fear or pressure, but self-respect.

You are worthy of love that adds to your life, not takes away. When thinking about your relationships, sometimes they are with people who may be somewhat narcissistic.

Recognizing narcissistic behavior can be especially painful because it often arrives wrapped in kindness, charm, or concern. At first, it feels like you've found someone who truly sees you, a partner who listens, praises, and makes you feel special. But beneath that initial warmth can lie a more complicated reality.

Over time, the sweetness starts to fade, revealing patterns that quietly erode your confidence and joy. You might notice subtle shifts: the way they dismiss your feelings, twist your words, or make you question your own memories. Maybe they blame you for things going wrong or turn every disagreement into a personal attack. These aren't just isolated moments, they're clues to a larger pattern of control and manipulation.

You might find yourself walking on eggshells, trying to avoid triggering their moods or walking the fine line between their approval and disapproval. The person who once seemed so caring can become someone who demands your constant attention but offers little kindness in return.

They may expect you to put their needs above your own, leaving you exhausted and doubting your worth. That invisible weight isn't your cross to bear. It's the burden of their need to dominate or control, and it's not a reflection of who you are.

Learning to spot these behaviors is an act of self-love and protection. It's about noticing when your sense of self starts to shrink or when your voice is silenced by fear of upsetting them. Setting clear boundaries, whether it's saying "no" to unfair demands or stepping away from emotional manipulation, isn't about pushing someone away.

It's about drawing a line that says, "I matter. My feelings matter. I deserve respect." Boundaries are the foundation of healing and the first step to reclaiming the bright, whole person you've always been beneath the hurt and confusion.

Remember, healing doesn't happen overnight, and recognizing these patterns is a courageous step. You are not alone in this. By honoring yourself, your needs, and your boundaries, you create space for genuine connection, one where love feels safe, nurturing, and real. You deserve nothing less.

CHAPTER 20

Choose With Confidence

Let me sit with you for a minute, not as an expert, not as someone who's figured it all out, but as someone who's walked through it too. Maybe your heart's been through a lot. Maybe you gave your best to someone who only took. Maybe you stayed longer than you knew you should, hoping things would change, hoping your love would be enough to fix what they wouldn't even try to heal.

Maybe you gave your time, your trust, your money, your whole spirit... and in return, you got distance. Or blame. Or silence. Maybe they accused you of things you'd never even imagine doing. Said things that cut deep. Projected their own wounds onto you and treated you like you were the one who needed fixing. I know how painful that is, to be misunderstood, misjudged, and mistreated by someone you once trusted with your heart.

And now here you are, trying to put the pieces back together. Maybe you're learning how to breathe again. Maybe you're trying to believe that love is still possible. Or maybe you're afraid to try, afraid that history will repeat itself and you'll end up back in that same place, wondering how you got there again.

I want you to know, I see you. I see the way your heart still wants to hope, even when it's tired. I've watched strong, brilliant, and kind-hearted people be used for their generosity and steadiness. I've seen beautiful souls lose their light, not because they were weak, but because they kept giving, long after someone stopped giving back.

From now on, you get to choose differently, not from fear, not from pressure, not from that voice in your head that says you're running out of time, but from a place of worth. Deep, quiet, unshakable worth.

You deserve someone who honors the path you've walked. Who respects your healing and doesn't see your strength as a threat? Someone who doesn't shrink in your light but stands beside it and shines with you. Someone who doesn't get jealous of your growth or punish you for having boundaries.

If anyone's ever made you feel like you were "too much," let me say this from my heart to yours: Your light is not too bright. Your truth is not too loud. Your love is not too deep. You're not asking for too much.

Just breathe. Ground yourself. And when you choose again, choose with open eyes and a heart that remembers everything it's learned. You are worthy of someone who shows up. Who listens. Who leans in when things get hard? Who never makes you question your value, because they already see it, clearly and completely.

You are ready for something real. And it's not only possible, but also already on its way.

CHAPTER 21

Reclaiming Your Joy After Hurt

I know what it's like to have your joy knocked out of you. Not just sadness, but that dull, aching kind of quiet where your heart forgets what it used to love. When someone you trusted hurts you, it can feel like a part of your light went with them. But I want you to hear this, and I hope it sinks in deep: your joy is still yours. It never left you. It's just been waiting patiently for you to come back to it.

Healing isn't about pretending the pain never happened. It's not about slapping on a smile or rushing to feel better so others won't worry. It's about learning to live again with grace, honesty, and a slower kind of strength. Cry when you need to. Laugh when you can. Breathe deeply. Give yourself full permission to take up space, even if you feel a little broken. That's not weakness, it's healing in motion.

Surround yourself with people who remind you who you are. Maybe it's your sister who always sees the spark in you, or a friend who texts you funny posts at midnight just to hear you laugh.

Maybe it's a cozy nook by the window where you read, a song you used to dance to, or the quiet of nature reminding you to trust the rhythm of things again.

Joy isn't found by avoiding what hurt you. It's found in the choice to rise, anyway. Some days it will come easy. Other days you'll have to reach for it like a flower turning toward light. But it's there. Always.

Let's talk about emotional maturity, not the kind that's loud or impressive, but the kind that makes you feel safe in someone's presence. That calm energy when someone listens without interrupting.

When they ask how you're feeling and really want to know. That's what we're looking for.

It shows up in the little moments: how he handles being told "no," how he treats the waiter, how he responds when things don't go his way. A mature person doesn't need to control the moment or fix everything.

They know how to sit with discomfort, how to apologize sincerely, and how to hold space for both your feelings and their own.

He won't play games with your heart. He won't ghost you to get the upper hand or use silence as punishment. Instead, he'll communicate, not perfectly, but honestly. He'll admit when he's wrong. He'll lean in when things get hard instead of running for the exit.

And this kind of maturity? It's magnetic. It builds trust in the quietest, most consistent ways. You'll feel it when he remembers the little things, when he asks follow-up questions, when he sees the messy parts of you and stays.

You deserve someone who's done the work, not someone who makes you do it for both of you. Emotional maturity doesn't mean being flawless. It means showing up, especially when it's uncomfortable. That's where love grows roots.

CHAPTER 22

Healing After Heartbreak

Heartbreak can bring even the strongest among us to our knees. When someone you love walks away or lets you down, it carves out a hollow space in your heart you never asked for. Here's a gentle truth to hold close: healing doesn't follow a schedule. There's no set timeline to feeling whole again, and no one has the right to rush your journey.

Some days, you'll feel okay, moving forward little by little. Other days, a song, a scent, or a memory will catch you off guard, and sadness washes over you. That's not failure, it's simply being human. Healing rarely moves in a straight line. It twists, loops, and dips, surprising you when you least expect it. Give yourself permission to take all the time you need, fully and without guilt.

Let go of the pressure to "bounce back" quickly. Healing isn't about proving strength to the world, it's about being tender with yourself as your soul slowly mends. If you need rest, rest deeply. If tears come, let them fall freely. And when laughter bubbles up unexpectedly, welcome it with open arms and an open heart. Take time to pray, to center yourself, and allow whatever emotions arise to flow through you.

One practice that has brought me peace may sound unusual but has been a balm for my heart: I write down what I'm feeling, every thought, every worry, every prayer asking God to take these burdens from my mind, heart, and soul. Then I read it back, tear the paper into pieces, burn it carefully on a cookie sheet, and bury the ashes. It feels like a sacred petition, a way to release years of pain and stress all at once. It works for me; it's been nothing short of a miracle.

After that, sometimes the best medicine is simply doing something gentle for yourself. Go see a movie, make some popcorn, or settle in with a favorite show at home. Give yourself permission to rest and breathe. Healing is a journey, and every small step matters.

The light inside you? It's not gone. It's just resting. When it's ready, it will shine again, warmer, softer, wiser, and brighter than before. There's no need to rush.

CHAPTER 23

Listening to Your Heart

Let's take a quiet moment together, just you and me. Sometimes, the most meaningful love story you'll ever write isn't the one you hope to find with someone else; it's the one you write for yourself. That story doesn't start in a dramatic moment, but in the quiet refrain of the day when you finally listen to that still, steady voice inside you. The voice that knows what you need, not to fix yourself or become someone else, but to come home to who you've always been.

One of the most healing things you can do is give your heart space to speak, not to perform or prove, but just to listen. Journaling is one of the most powerful tools for this. There's something sacred about putting pen to paper and letting your thoughts, feelings, and memories spill out, uncensored and unfiltered. It's not about the "right" words; it's about being honest with yourself.

Years ago, my therapist encouraged me to write whatever came to mind, no rules, no pressure. I filled pages without knowing where the words came from. My hand uncovered feelings and memories my heart had tried to bury, pain, fear, patterns I hadn't fully faced. As those words poured out, understanding grew.

Slowly, I saw the connections: why I felt certain ways, why I held back, why I stayed small or silent. It wasn't easy, but it changed everything. It brought clarity, strength, and a deeper sense of myself. From that place, I grew softer, stronger, and ready to show up fully in life.

I share this because I believe in the power of listening to yourself. Give your heart the space it needs to speak without fear or judgment. Healing doesn't have to be perfect or neat, it just needs to be honest. And when you allow that truth, peace will rise inside you.

You deserve that peace. You deserve to know yourself deeply. You deserve to love the person you find there.

Let that be the story you begin writing today.

CHAPTER 24

Choosing to Love Yourself

Ask yourself gentle questions: What brings me
peace? When do I feel most alive? What parts of
me have I silenced to keep others comfortable?
The more you write, the more you'll hear your
own inner voice, sometimes buried so deep it
takes time to uncover.

As you grow closer to yourself, you'll naturally
become more thoughtful about who you let close.
That's not being guarded, it's wisdom. You
deserve people, romantic or not, who respect you.
Who honors your boundaries? Who speaks
kindly, even when upset. Who listens without
turning your feelings into a debate or dismissal?

Your emotions are safe to express. You are not
"too much." Your sensitivity is a strength, not a
flaw. Your boundaries are sacred, not negotiable.
Anyone worth your time will recognize that.

On days you doubt yourself, when you're still
healing, or uncertain about the future, speak
gently to your soul: "I am allowed to be whole and

still growing. I am enough, even as I become." These aren't just affirmations, they're lifelines anchoring you to your truth when life pulls you away.

Listen to your heart when it says, "I need rest." You don't owe your energy to anyone who drains it. It's okay to pause, step back, and protect your peace, even if others don't understand. Caring for your emotional well-being isn't selfish, it's sacred.

Nourish your soul with simple acts: a walk in nature, quiet music, or creative moments that light you up. When you're nourished, the people and relationships you attract will mirror that same love and care.

This journey is yours alone. There's no rush, no race, no "right time" to finish healing or find love. Every step you take toward your true self draws you closer to people who see and cherish the real you. You don't have to perform to be loved, you just need to be authentic.

When you need a reminder of something greater, hold close these words from Psalm 37:4

"Delight yourself in the Lord, and he will give you the desires of your heart."

This beautiful promise reminds us that true joy and fulfillment begin when we find our deepest satisfaction in something steady, something unshakable. When you delight yourself in the Lord, that source of unconditional love and wisdom, you open a wellspring of peace within your soul that no circumstance can shake.

That peace? It's your birthright. It's not something you have to earn or prove. It's not a reward for being strong or perfect. It's the quiet, steady presence inside you that whispers calm when the world feels chaotic. It's the soft glow that gently lights your way through heartbreak, confusion, and uncertainty.

Because here's the truth: peace is the lens through which all love must be viewed. It's the filter that helps you see clearly whether a relationship nourishes your soul or depletes your spirit. When you protect that peace, when you hold it sacred, you set a powerful boundary around your heart. You're saying, "I will not settle for anything less than love that feels like home."

Guarding your peace means choosing what feels safe, what feels true, and what honors your worth. It means pausing when something doesn't feel right. It means trusting your intuition over empty promises or charming words. It means knowing that your well-being matters just as much as anyone else's.

And when you delight in the Lord, when you center yourself in that unchanging love, the desires of your heart will align with what is best for you, not just what feels good in the moment, but what builds a foundation of lasting joy.

So, carry this promise with you every day. Let it anchor you when doubt creeps in. Let it remind you that you are worthy of love that lifts, steadies, and blesses you deeply.

Your peace is precious. Protect it fiercely. Guard it gently. And let it be the sacred measure by which you welcome real love into your life.

Take these tools as your compass. Anchor yourself in truth, self-respect, and quiet strength. You are worthy of love that feels like peace, a love that honors your whole being and invites you to grow into even more of yourself. But that love always begins with the one you give yourself.

Thank you for walking this path with me.

Choosing yourself, truly and fully, is one of the bravest, most powerful acts of love you can give. It's not always easy. Sometimes it means saying no when your heart wants to say yes. Sometimes it means standing alone when all you want is to be held. Sometimes it means facing old wounds you thought were healed.

But through it all, you learn this life-changing truth: you are already enough, just as you are. No need to prove it. No need to change.

Love was never meant to complete you. That's a myth. Real love sees your wholeness and honors it. The right person will recognize your light, your depth, and your growth, and cherish it as sacred.

Wherever you are now, take a deep breath. Be kind to yourself. Let go of the rush. Fill your life with what makes you feel safe, strong, and peaceful. Celebrate the small wins. Sit with your feelings, even the hard ones; they are part of healing.

You deserve a love that feels like peace, that brings laughter without anxiety, that lets you rest because you're safe to be fully yourself. That love is possible, and worth every step.

The road may have been rough. You may have had to pause, rebuild, and reroute. That doesn't mean you're broken. It means you're wise. Your heart knows more than you think. Trust it. Trust yourself.

When real love comes, it won't need chasing or fixing. It will be steady, clear, and true. Until then, keep shining. Keep being you. Keep showing up for yourself.

About the Author

Tricia Greenwood is first and foremost an author, songwriter, and artist whose creative spirit shines through everything she does. With over forty years as a skilled hair designer, Tricia's journey has always been about more than style; it's been about people and hoping for their happiness.

Behind the chair in her intimate private salon, she listens deeply to the stories, struggles, and hopes of countless women and men. What started as a career in beauty blossomed into a lifelong calling to understand and uplift the human spirit.

Blending her passion for creativity with a keen interest in psychology and emotional wellness, Tricia has become a trusted voice on self-worth, love, and the quiet power of making wise, courageous choices.

She is the author of *Beautiful Thinking: Wisdom, Courage and Grace* and *Frazzle to Dazzle: How to Not Be a Victim of an Inexperienced Hairdresser*, both available on Amazon.

As a singer-songwriter, a vocal coach, and storyteller, Tricia uses every creative gift she possesses to remind people of their inherent dignity and value.

This book is no exception; it is a heartfelt conversation, a gentle reflection, and a warm invitation to step bravely into the fullness of real love.

Because, as Tricia believes, true love doesn't just happen, it's chosen, nurtured, and built on a foundation of truth.

A Note from the Author

Thank you for spending time with this book.
If something in these pages speaks to your heart,

I hope you'll carry it with you and share it with
someone else who needs it too. Your words may
help someone else discover exactly what they
need in this divided world we live in today.

May you always choose love with wisdom, wait
with courage, and believe in the kind of
connection that is real and lasting.

Please consider leaving a review.

With all my heart,

Tricia

www.ingramcontent.com/pod-product-compliance
Lightning Source LLC
Chambersburg PA
CBHW051225120626
46547CB00013B/1512